INVEST KIDS™

HOW CREDIT CARDS WORK

Gillian Houghton

PowerKiDS press™

New York

Published in 2009 by The Rosen Publishing Group, Inc.
29 East 21st Street, New York, NY 10010

First Edition

Editor: Joanne Randolph
Book Design: Julio Gil
Photo Researcher: Jessica Gerweck

Photo Credits: Cover, p. 18 © Michael Krasowitz/Getty Images; back cover, pp. 6, 10, 13, 14, 17 Shutterstock.com; p. 5 © Andersen Ross/Getty Images; p. 9 © www.iStockphoto.com/Eugene Choi; p. 21 © Richard Elliott/Getty Images.

Library of Congress Cataloging-in-Publication Data

Houghton, Gillian.
  How credit cards work / Gillian Houghton. — 1st ed.
      p. cm. — (Invest kids)
  Includes index.
  ISBN 978-1-4358-2773-8 (library binding) — ISBN 978-1-4358-3208-4 (pbk.)
ISBN 978-1-4358-3214-5 (6-pack)
  1. Credit cards—Juvenile literature. I. Title.
  HG3755.7.H68 2009
  332.7'65—dc22
                                    2008037774

Manufactured in the United States of America

Contents

Hello, Credit!

Credit cards are a common form of **payment**. The cardholder, or person with a credit card, can use it at shops, movie theaters, the post office, the train station, and many other places. Credit cards are safer and easier to carry than cash. They are small, lightweight, and hard to break. Credit cards are an easy way to pay when you do not have cash on hand. It is important to use credit cards wisely, though.

Even though you cannot use a credit card yet, it is important to learn how a credit card works and how to use one safely. This book will tell you what you need to know about paying on credit.

This family is paying for their dinner using a credit card. A credit card can be an easy way to pay for something when you do not want to carry a lot of cash.

All credit cards must be the same size, a little more than 3 inches (8 cm) long and 2 inches (5 cm) wide.

What Is a Credit Card?

A credit card is issued, or given out, by a bank. On the front of the card, the bank prints your name, your **account number**, the date the credit card **expires**, and the **logo** of the company that made the card. There is also a **microchip** on it. These are different ways of setting your card apart from every other credit card.

A credit card lets you buy things with a promise to pay the bank back for them over time. The merchant, or person who sells things, takes your card because the bank that issues the card will pay her.

What Is Credit?

The word "credit" means a number of things. In the case of credit cards, credit is generally a **loan** given by one person, called the lender, to another person, called the borrower. The borrower agrees to pay back the amount of money borrowed plus extra money, called interest, over time. The total money the borrower owes is called debt.

If the borrower pays the debt on time, he is said to have good credit. A borrower with good credit is more likely to get another loan because the lender can trust the borrower to pay back the debt on time.

You can talk to a bank manager about ways to improve your credit. Plan how you will spend and save so you do not end up with too much debt from using a credit card.

This is a credit card reader. There is generally a slot through which the card can be pulled, and there are buttons on the top for anything that needs to be entered by hand.

How Does a Credit Card Work?

When you use your credit card, you borrow money from the bank that issued the card to pay a merchant. The merchant pulls your card through a reader. The reader is a machine that reads the information, or facts, stored in the **magnetic strip** on the back of the card.

The reader talks to the bank through a telephone line. The bank makes sure your card is real, then allows the **purchase**. The reader then prints out a **receipt**. By signing the receipt, you agree to pay the charge. The bank pays the merchant right away, and you pay the bank over time.

The Numbers on the Card

On the front of every credit card is a long list of numbers. This number is a **code**. If you know how to read it, the code will tell you a lot!

The first number stands for the credit card company or system that made the card. For example, one common credit card company, MasterCard, is set apart by the number 5. Generally, the next two to five numbers on the card tell you which bank issued it. Next is your account number. This number sets your card apart from every other card.

You need a credit card to shop at most online stores. You type in the card number, the expiration date, and sometimes a code from the back of the card.

It is important to look over your statement to make sure it is right each month. If you see any problems, call the credit card company right away.

The Statement

Once each month, the bank that issued your credit card sends you a statement. A statement is a list of every time you used your credit card and how much money you spent. It also tells you what you paid back last month. When you get your statement, read it carefully. Did you make each of the purchases listed? Can you **afford** everything you bought?

At the bottom of the statement is the total amount of money spent, called the balance. You must pay part or all of this balance, or the bank may charge you extra money.

Interest and Perks

Generally, if you do not have the money to pay the full balance, the bank will charge you interest. Interest is an extra cost for you. You must pay the bank a **percentage** of the money you owe, plus pay back the money you spent. Most of the time, if you pay the full balance each month, the bank will not charge you interest.

Many credit cards come with perks, or gifts. Some credit cards give cardholders a point for every dollar they spend. These points can be spent, like money, for other purchases. Other credit cards give cardholders money back.

Choose a credit card that charges low interest and offers useful perks. Some credit cards will give money back for every dollar you spend at a store buying things you need.

Merchants pay banks for the right to take payment in the form of credit cards. Merchants know they are likely to make more sales if they let people use credit cards.

Why Do Banks Give Credit?

Banks are businesses. This means that they sell services to their **customers** in order to make money. They loan money to their credit card customers because they know that many cardholders will not pay it back right away. When this happens, the bank will charge the cardholder interest.

Banks also charge cardholders who spend more than their credit limit, or the amount of money they are allowed to charge each month. There are many other kinds of fees, or costs, each month. These fees add up to a lot of money, which allows banks to do quite well.

Keeping Your Credit Safe

On the back of your credit card, there is space to sign your name as you would on a receipt. Sign your card as soon as you get it. Some cards are now being made with a picture of the cardholder on the front. These things make it harder for someone else to use your card.

There are a few other steps you can take to stay safe. Save your receipts in a safe place. Make sure you get your card back after every purchase. Read your statement each month to see if you have been charged for purchases you did not make.

When your credit card statement comes, pull out your receipts and make sure that they match with the charges on your statement. Then be sure to pay your bill on time!

Use Your Card with Care

Many people have a lot of credit card debt. They buy things that they cannot afford, and the card issuer charges more interest every month as the balance grows. These people have bad credit, which makes it harder for them to borrow money for important purchases, such as a home.

It is very hard to get free from a lot of debt. For this reason, it is important to use a credit card carefully. Before you buy something, ask yourself whether you can afford it. Do not make purchases that you cannot pay back right away. Be smart, and stay out of debt.

GLOSSARY

account number (uh-KOWNT NUM-ber) A number that sets each credit card apart from the others.

afford (uh-FORD) To have enough money to pay for something.

code (KOHD) Something that stands for something else, or numbers and letters that hold facts about something.

customers (KUS-tuh-murz) The people who buy goods or services.

expires (ik-SPY-urz) Comes to an end or is no longer good.

loan (LOHN) Money given to a person that must be paid back later.

logo (LOH-goh) A picture or something that stands for a person or group.

magnetic strip (mag-NEH-tik STRIP) A part on a card that holds data, or facts.

microchip (MY-kroh-chip) A small computer that holds data, or facts, about something.

payment (PAY-ment) An amount of money paid for a good or service.

percentage (per-SEN-tij) An amount based on the total amount. One percent is one part of 100.

purchase (PUR-chus) Something that is bought.

receipt (rih-SEET) A printed list of what has been bought.

INDEX

WEB SITES

Due to the changing nature of Internet links, PowerKids Press has developed an online list of Web sites related to the subject of this book. This site is updated regularly. Please use this link to access the list:
www.powerkidslinks.com/ikids/credit/